JUNGLES

Written by **Jenny Wood**

Consultant Roger Hammond
Director of Living Earth

SCHOLASTIC INC.
New York Toronto London Auckland Sydney

ISBN 0-590-61963-2

Copyright © 1991 by Two-Can Publishing Ltd. Text copyright © 1991 by Jenny Wood. All rights reserved. Published by Scholastic Inc., 555 Broadway, New York, NY 10012, by arrangement with Two-Can Publishing Ltd.

12 11 10 9 8 7 6 5 4 3 2 1   6 7 8 9/9 0 1/0

Printed in U.S.A.   14

First Scholastic printing, March 1996

Photographic Credits:
Cover (front) Tony Stone (back) Nature Photographers; p.5 Ardea; p.8 (top) Ardea (bottom) Bruce Coleman; p.9 (top) Bruce Coleman (bottom) Survival Anglia p.10 (top) Frank Lane (bottom) Frank Lane; p.11 Survival Anglia; p.12 (top) Bruce Coleman (bottom) Bruce Coleman; p.13 Hutchinson; p.14 (top) Frank Lane (bottom) Frank Lane p.15 (top) Frank Lane (bottom) Frank Lane; p.16 Hutchinson; p.17 (top) Survival Anglia (bottom) Survival Anglia; p.18 Hutchinson; p.19 Hutchinson; p.20 Oxford Scientific Films; p.22 Planet Earth Pictures; p.23 Mark Edwards.

Illustration Credits:
All illustrations by Francis Mosley except p.24-28 Jon Davis/Linden Artists.

CONTENTS

All words marked in **bold** can be found in the glossary.

WHAT IS A JUNGLE?

A jungle is an area of densely packed trees and plants. The word is usually used to describe tropical rainforests. These forests lie near the Equator, the imaginary line around the center of the Earth. Rain falls almost every day, and the temperature varies very little between the hottest and the coldest month. Tropical rainforests are packed with all kinds of vegetation, from trees and creepers to shrubs and brightly colored flowers. About half the world's **species** of plants and animals are found in tropical rainforests.

▶ Tropical rainforest in Australia

Emergent Layer

Canopy Layer

Understory or 'middle' Layer

Shrub Layer

Forest floor

◀ The layers of vegetation in a tropical rainforest.
Emergent layer Some trees grow as tall as 200'.
Canopy layer The trees in this layer grow from 98' to 151' tall. Their tops or crowns form a roof of leaves over the forest
Understory or 'middle' layer The shorter trees that grow beneath the canopy form this layer. They reach a height of about 63'.
Shrub layer This layer consists of short, woody plants which have more than one stem. The tall trees filter out so much sunlight that few shrubs are able to grow.
Forest floor Very little sunlight reaches the forest floor. A thick covering of leaves, twigs and animal droppings, as well as the remains of dead animals and plants, builds up.

ALL AROUND THE WORLD

Tropical rainforests cover about seven per cent of the surface of the Earth. They occupy large areas of Central and South America, West Africa, and Asia. Smaller areas occur in Australia and in Papua New Guinea. All tropical rainforests are similar, but different animal and plant species are found in each of the different continents.

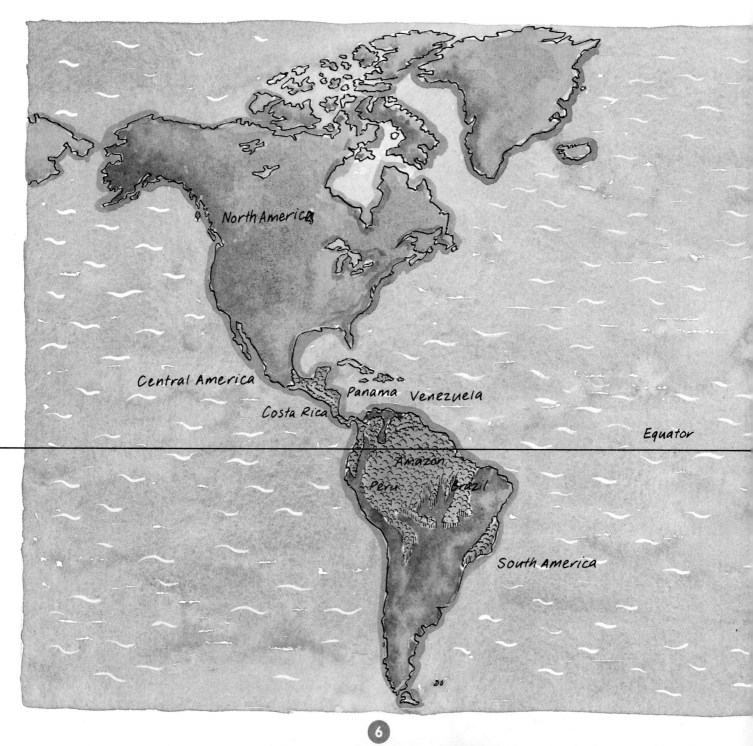

The world's tropical rainforests are in great danger. They are being cut down to provide timber and firewood, and to make room for homes, roads, farms and factories. Some areas are being cleared to allow oil and valuable **minerals** such as gold to be mined. Scientists estimate that about 42 million acres are now being destroyed every year. The **habitats** of thousands of species of animals and plants have already vanished. The way of life of many rainforest peoples is also under threat from these changes.

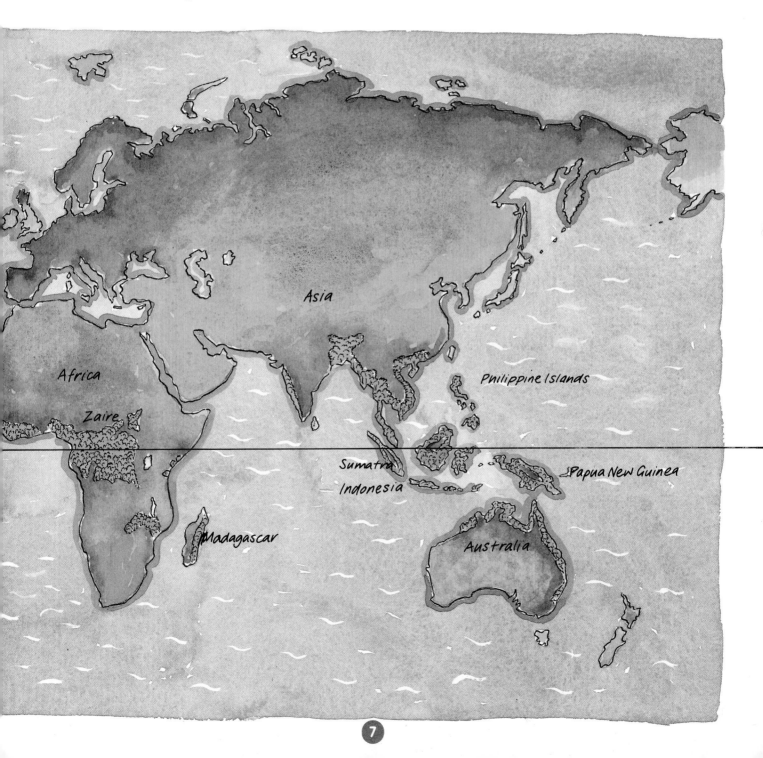

CREEPERS AND CLIMBERS

Trees and plants thrive in the warm, damp conditions of a tropical rainforest. There is always a tree or plant bearing fruit, and the forest is always green.

Most tropical rainforest trees are **evergreens**. They only have branches near the tops of their trunks. The leaves are dark green and tough, with pointed drip-tips to let the rainwater run off. Climbing plants called lianas loop from tree to tree like huge ropes tying the whole forest together. Plants like ferns, mosses, orchids and **bromeliads** grow on the trunks and branches of living trees.

▲ Rainforests contain many interesting plants. Some of these, such as palms and orchids, have become popular house plants.

◄ In tropical rainforests, plants known as **epiphytes** grow high on the trees, close to the sunlight. They get food and moisture from the air.

► The roots of some tropical rainforest trees form wide, spreading growths around the tree's base. These buttress roots help keep the tree upright.

◀ The pitcher plant feeds off insects, which are trapped in its tube-shaped leaves. A sweet smell given off by tiny glands inside the top edge of the leaves attracts insects to the plant. When an insect lands, it is trapped by the plant's bristly hairs. It then slides down into the tube.

DID YOU KNOW?

● There are more kinds of trees in a tropical rainforest than in any other area of the world. In one section of rainforest in South America, scientists counted 179 different species of trees in an area the size of a large garden.

● About 155,000 of the 250,000 known species of plants are found in tropical rainforests.

● The giant rafflesia produces the largest flowers of any known plant. Unfortunately, the flowers usually smell very unpleasant.

● A scientist at Harvard University has worked out that it would take 25,000 scientists their whole working lives to record all the known **flora and fauna** of the world's tropical rainforests.

ROAMING THE JUNGLE

Many of the animals in a tropical rainforest spend their lives high up in the trees, where there are always flowers, leaves, fruit and nuts to eat. They have developed ways of moving through the canopy in search of food. Some, like monkeys, are very agile and climb well. Others, such as flying **lemurs** and flying squirrels, are able to glide from tree to tree. Snakes loop themselves around the branches,

▲ Tree frogs eat insects and other small animals. Many can change color to blend in with their surroundings. Some male tree frogs make a high-pitched squeak to attract females. In order to make this sound, the tree frog's throat swells up like a balloon.

▼ The tiger hunts alone, stalking its prey slowly and carefully. It kills its prey with a single blow of its forepaw.

while tree frogs have sticky pads on their feet to stop them falling.

Larger animals like antelope, deer and **tapirs**, as well as small rodents, roam the forest floor. They feed on roots, seeds, leaves, and fruit which has fallen to the ground. Some animals, such as gorillas, live on the ground as well as in the trees.

Although many tropical rainforest animals are plant eaters, or herbivores, others, such as jaguars and tigers, are carnivores. Carnivores hunt and kill other animals for food. The hunted

▲ Sloths, which live in the rainforests of South America, spend most of their time hanging upside-down from branches. Their claws grip the branches so securely that they can fall asleep in this position. Sloths often carry their babies on their bellies.

animals have to be on constant look-out against possible danger.

The destruction of so many areas of tropical rainforest means that many of the animals which live there are now in danger of **extinction**. Orangutans, jaguars and gorillas are some of the rainforest animals under threat.

THE COLORFUL CANOPY

Most tropical rainforest birds live high up in the canopy, where there is plenty of food. Hawks and eagles soar above the emergent layer, swooping down from time to time to snatch up other birds, bats, and even monkeys. Many tropical rainforest birds have very brightly colored feathers. Although you might think this would make them easy to spot against the green of the trees, in fact the bright colors act as a kind of camouflage. The bright spots of color can easily be mistaken for flowers or fruit.

Male bowerbirds, found in the tropical rainforests of New Guinea and Australia, build beautiful bowers or shelters in which to court their mates. The bowers are built of grass, moss, twigs and creepers, and are often decorated with brightly colored feathers, berries, shells and flowers.

▶ Tropical rainforest birds have developed different ways of feeding. Macaws use their strong beaks to crack nuts like brazil nuts with no difficulty.

◀ Hummingbirds' wings beat so fast, it is almost impossible for the human eye to detect any movement at all. The smallest member of the hummingbird family measures only 2" from the tip of its bill to the tip of its tail! Its body is about the same size as that of a large bumble-bee, and it weighs less than .01 oz. Hummingbirds have long, slender bills and long tongues, which allow them to suck nectar from the center of even the deepest tube-shaped flowers.

◀ An African gray parrot enjoying a meal. Like most other types of parrot and macaw, the African gray is able to hold its food in one foot and bite pieces off, similar to the way in which humans might eat a sandwich! The parrot keeps its balance by curling its other foot around the branch. A parrots's foot has four toes, two of which lie to the front, the other two to the rear, so it is easy for the bird to grip the branch tightly and securely.

THE TINIEST CREATURES

Scientists believe that up to 80% of all the world's insect species live only in tropical rainforests. A recent study of a 2.5 acre area of a rainforest in Peru found 41,000 different types of insect species living in the canopy alone. There may be between 1 million and 10 million insect species still undiscovered, so, if you spent a day in a tropical rainforest collecting insects, you would probably find one that no one else had ever seen.

Insects are fascinating creatures. Most of them smell with their **antennae**, some taste with their feet. Some have no eyes; others have five eyes or more. Many are very strong – the ant, for example, can lift an object 50 times heavier than its own body weight.

▲ This insect is a type of giant weevil. Its antennae are positioned half-way down its long nose, at the end of which is it's mouth. A female weevil uses her long nose to drill a hole in which to lay her eggs.

◀ Leafcutter ants cut pieces of leaves from trees, plants and shrubs. They carry the leaves back to their nest, holding them above their heads. Inside the nest, the ants chew the leaves into a pulp which is then left to rot. The ants feed on a fungus which grows on the rotting pulp.

Insects are great survivors, too. They can live in places that are too small for other animals and they need little food. An insect's skeleton is on the outside of its body, which protects it against injury and prevents its body losing moisture. Being able to fly makes it easier to find food and escape from enemies.

◀ This crab spider can disguise itself by changing the color of its body to match the color of the flower blossom in which it is crawling. Scientists call spiders arachnids because they are different from insects. They have eight legs, whereas insects have only six.

▼ The bright colors of this young grasshopper suggest that it might be a poisonous insect. This stops enemies such as spiders and beetles approaching.

LIVING IN THE JUNGLE

Some tribes of people live deep in the jungle, just as their ancestors have done for generations. Many of them farm using a method called slash-and-burn cultivation. First. they chop down trees to clear a space in the forest. They burn the trees and plant seeds among the ashes. The crops grow quickly in the warm, moist ground. After a few years, the thin layer of soil

▼ Some houses, like this one in Indonesia, are built on stilts if the ground is swampy.

● The Efe people , a **pygmy** tribe who live in the Ituri Forest in Zaire, build huts from saplings and leaves. The saplings are driven into the soft ground, then bent over into a dome shape. Branches are woven through the bent saplings and the whole framework is covered with leaves.

● Some people who live in the Amazon rainforest build shelters big enough to house a whole community. The shelters are the shape of wheels, with an open center.

● The Kraho Indians of Brazil arrange their villages in the shape of a wheel. The houses are built around the edge of the wheel. Pathways lead to the center, where the villagers hold meetings.

loses its goodness and crops no longer grow well. The people move to another area and begin again.

Rainforest people also gather fruit and plants from the forest. They hunt animals using blowpipes, poisoned darts, bows and arrows or spears.

Rainforest people build shelters which can be put up quickly, when the group arrives in a new area.

◀ Embera Indians in Panama grinding manioc plant roots. The roots contain poison so must be ground and washed before they can be eaten.

▼ A Penan man spearing fish in Sarawak, Malaysia.

CHANGING WAYS

The world's population has more than doubled in the last 40 years, and is continuing to increase at the rate of 155 people every minute. This dramatic rise causes enormous problems. People need somewhere to live and work, and they need food to eat. Huge areas of tropical rainforest have been cut down to provide areas for settlement and farming. In Brazil, for example, over a million people have been resettled in cleared

In some tropical rainforests, loggers remove only certain trees or species of tree, rather than simply felling the whole area. But the heavy machinery used causes enormous damage. In Asia, for example, it is estimated that for every ten trees felled deliberately, another thirteen are seriously damaged.

rainforest areas. But these **colonization** schemes often fail because the soil is too poor to allow the crops to grow well.

The more people there are in the world, the more demand there is for goods such as furniture, window-frames and doors made from **tropical hardwood** such as mahogany and teak. Tropical rainforests lie mostly in the poorer countries of the world, and these countries can make a lot of money by selling timber to the world's richer countries. Other rainforest areas have been cut down to clear space for oilfields and mines.

▼ A section of the Amazon forest, cleared for settlement.

The effect of all of these changes on the ways of life of many rainforest peoples has been enormous. The destruction of the forests has made it more difficult for them to survive by hunting and farming. Many of the animals and plants that they relied upon for food have died out. Huge roads have been built through the forests, and settlers, miners, **loggers**, scientists and even tourists now have access to areas which were once remote. These newcomers have brought diseases to the rainforest peoples, against which they have no resistance.

▼ The Amazon forest in South America is the largest tropical rainforest in the world. Over 6,214 miles of road now runs through the forest.

WHAT USE ARE JUNGLES?

It is not hard to guess that a piece of wooden furniture may have been made from a tropical rainforest tree. However, did you know that golf balls, nail polish, deodorant, toothpaste, chewing gum, shampoo and the glue on postage stamps are all made from or contain materials obtained from the world's tropical rainforests? Many of the foods you eat have been developed from tropical rainforest plants. When you are ill, the medicine the doctor

▼ A South American Indian collects latex to make rubber.

gives you may contain plant extracts and the hot water bottle that keeps you warm began its life as a milky juice which comes from the rubber tree.

Many of the foods we eat no longer come directly from the tropical rainforests, but are grown on large **plantations**.

Rainforest peoples have made medicines from plants for hundreds of years. It is only fairly recently though that scientists have discovered how useful tropical rainforest plants may be in producing life-saving drugs which can be used to treat people all over the world. At least 1,400 plants found in tropical rainforests are now believed to offer possible treatments against cancer.

ROTTING LEAVES

The forest floor is covered with leaves, twigs, animal droppings and the remains of dead animals. These waste materials break down and decay quickly in the moist heat, providing food for animals, insects and plants. Try this experiment to see how leaves rot.

You will need:
- Two margarine tubs (one with a lid)
- Fresh, dry leaves
- Wet soil

1 Put some of the leaves in each tub.

2 Add wet soil to one container, and pack it around the leaves. Put the lid on this container.

3 Look at the containers every few weeks. The ones in the wet soil will slowly begin to rot.

JUNGLES IN DANGER

If the world's tropical rainforests are to be saved from total destruction, many people believe that action must be taken now. Scientists need to find ways of supplying timber without destroying entire forests. They need to develop ways of putting goodness back into the soil left bare by forest clearance, and to organize **reforestation** schemes.

Politicians and business people need to begin to cooperate with the native rainforest peoples, who know and understand the forests. People in rich countries need to reduce their demand for tropical hardwood and look for alternative materials.

Unless something is done quickly, all the possible benefits to the world will be lost.

The world's climate may change, too. The destruction of the tropical rainforests has added to the growing amount of carbon dioxide gas in the atmosphere. Carbon dioxide and other gases are causing an alarming change in the world's climate. This change is known as **global warming** or the **greenhouse effect.**

▶ Slash-and-burn cultivation used to be confined to small areas of the rainforest. Today, however, huge areas are burnt down by big companies.

◀ Every year, an area of the Amazon rainforest is flooded for six months or more. The waters can rise to a height of about 30 ft. Only the tops of the tallest trees remain above water. Others are completely under water – but they go on growing! Normally, floods destroy trees, but in this area of the Amazon, when the flood waters go down, the trees have suffered no harm. This flooded forest is a unique habitat, with a huge variety of wildlife. It, too, is under threat.

JUNGLE RESCUE

The engine of the tiny plane coughed, sputtered and stopped. O'Reilly and Jackson looked at each other in utter horror.

"Fasten your seatbelts," the pilot shouted, as the plane began to lose height. He peered anxiously through the windshield, searching for a suitable landing spot. He could see nothing but trees. The jungle stretched like a giant green carpet as far as the eye could see.

The jungle seemed to rush up towards them. Then, with a splintering crash, the plane ploughed through the tree tops, smashing through the branches until if finally came to a halt. It hung for a few seconds then slid, nose first, towards the ground. There was complete silence.

O'Reilly unfastened his seat-belt and looked around. The plane was wedged at an impossible angle between two giant trees. A huge branch had ripped through the thin fuselage and was sticking into the cabin. O'Reilly became aware that his fellow passenger was groaning in pain. Hauling himself across the crazily angled floor, O'Reilly examined his companion. Jackson's leg was broken.

O'Reilly spent several minutes finding the first aid kit and then two reasonably straight branches for splints. He strapped up the leg as best he could and gave Jackson some pain-killers. Then he groped his way to the cockpit. The pilot was unconscious.

O'Reilly returned to the cabin.

"The pilot's out cold and the radio's broken," he explained. "It'll be hours before anyone misses us, let alone sends out a rescue party."

Jackson nodded stiffly.

"I'll go for help," continued O'Reilly. "I spotted a clearing not far away as we were coming down. I'll be as quick as I can."

Making Jackson as comfortable as he could, O'Reilly climbed out of the plane and grabbed hold of a creeper to help him down through the trees. Within minutes, his shirt was soaked with sweat from the sticky heat. Dust and dirt stuck to his damp skin. Branches whipped him as he forced his way downwards until red scratches covered his arms and face.

When he reached the jungle floor he found to his surprise that it was quite clear. A thick layer of leaves and animal droppings covered it, but few plants barred his way. With one last glance at the plane, he set off in the direction of the clearing.

In places the trees nearly blotted out the sun, reducing the light to a green twilight. This made walking very difficult, as he could not see fallen branches, roots or ditches. He stumbled and tripped in these dark places. Swarms of insects buzzed around his face, moving only when he brushed them away with his hand, to return moments later, thicker than ever.

All around, he could hear the sounds of the jungle. Birds and monkeys chattered loudly and branches creaked and swayed. From time to time, he caught a glimpse of larger animals between the trees, but they stayed out of his way.

O'Reilly stopped to rest when he reached the river. After hours of walking, he was exhausted.

He picked a piece of fruit off a nearby tree and ate it before going on, following the river bank.

The bank was much harder to walk on than the forest floor. A tangle of roots and slimy mud covered it. Once, O'Reilly slipped and had to grab a branch to stop himself tumbling into the water. As his foot splashed on the surface of the water, he saw the long, low form of an alligator sliding into the water. From then on, he walked more carefully.

Then, at last, he saw a flickering light through the trees. It was the campfire in a logging camp. With a last desperate burst of energy, O'Reilly staggered into the circle of firelight. The loggers started up in surprise at the sight of his scarecrow figure. O'Reilly stammered out his story.

Within minutes the logging company's helicopter had taken off. In spite of O'Reilly's accurate directions, the jungle seemed to have swallowed the wrecked plane. The helicopter criss-crossed the trees, its powerful searchlight probing the darkness below. It was over an hour before the helicopter was finally hovering over the crashed plane, while the crew winched up the injured pilot and passenger. A radio signal crackled the news to the logging camp, where O'Reilly now sat staring into the firelight, exhausted. Only when he heard that Jackson and the pilot were safe, did he at last close his eyes and fall into a deep sleep.

TRUE OR FALSE?

Which of these facts are true and which ones are false?
If you have read this book carefully, you will know the answers.

1 The Amazon forest in South America is the largest tropical rainforest in the world.

2 About a quarter of the world's species of plants and animals live in tropical rainforests.

3 All jungle animals are herbivores (plant-eaters).

4 Most tropical rainforest trees have branches only near the top of their trunks.

5 Many tropical rainforest plants are used to cure illness and disease.

6 The climate in a tropical rainforest is cold and damp.

7 Epiphytes are a type of spider.

8 An ant can lift an object 50 times heavier than its own body weight.

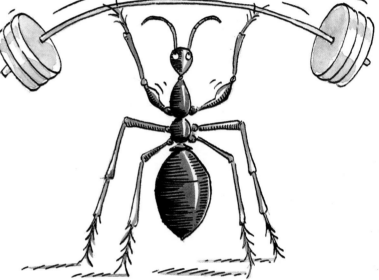

9 Many of the foods you eat have been developed from tropical rainforest plants.

10 Few tropical rainforest birds have very brightly colored feathers.

11 The canopy forms a roof of leaves over the forest.

12 The waste materials on the forest floor provide food for animals, insects, trees and plants.

GLOSSARY

Antennae are the parts of an insect's body which it uses for touching and feeling other objects. Antennae are positioned on an insect's head.

Bromeliads are members of a large family of plants, most of which grow in the tropical rainforests of Central and South America. Most bromeliads are epiphytes, and have long sword-shaped leaves.

Colonization means sending people from one area of a country to another or from one country to another, so that they can build homes and form a new town or settlement.

Epiphytes are plants which grow on other plants and take their food and water from the air.

Evergreens are trees which have green leaves all year round. Evergreens do shed their old leaves, but they form new ones first.

Extinction means dying out. A species of animal or plant becomes extinct when every one of its kind has died. Species usually become extinct because their habitat is destroyed and they have lost their source of food.

Flora and fauna is a phrase used to describe the plant and animal species found in a particular area.

Global warming and Greenhouse effect are phrases used to describe the warming of the Earth by gases which have been released into the atmosphere. These gases trap heat, and so the Earth warms up. Nobody is quite sure what the final effect will be, but if the Earth continues to warm up, the ice at the Poles will begin to melt. This will make the sea levels rise and eventually a lot of land could disappear underwater.

Habitat is the word used to describe the natural home of a plant, animal, insect or person.

Lemurs are monkey-like animals which are found on the island of Madagascar. Most lemurs live in trees. Some are active only at night.

Loggers are people who are employed to cut down trees.

Minerals are substances other than plants which can be dug from the ground.

Plantation is a large area of land given over to the growing of a particular crop.

Pygmy is the word used to describe a group of native African people who live in the tropical rainforests. Pygmies are usually between 4' and 4' 6" tall. They also live in parts of Asia.

Reforestation means planting trees over a bare area of ground which was once covered by forest.

Species is the word used to describe a group of animals or plants which are alike in certain ways.

Tapir is a kind of mammal which looks rather like a giant pig but is related to the rhinoceros.

Tropical hardwood is the phrase used to describe the wood obtained from many tropical rainforest trees. Mahogany, ebony, teak and rosewood are all tropical hardwoods.

INDEX